THE AFFORDABLE KETO MEAL PREP COOKBOOK

5-Ingredients or Less Quick & Easy Meal Prep
Recipes on the Ketogenic Diet

ISBN: 9798651936502

TABLE OF CONTENTS

KETO DIET GUIDE

Welcome, and congratulations on taking another step in your ketogenic diet (or keto diet) journey. This diet is more than just another trend; it is a lifestyle. This book provides recipes for every moment of the day. All of these recipes are five ingredients or less (excluding salt and pepper, and butter and oils used for cooking).

What is the Keto Diet?

The Keto Diet is a plan that increases the amount of fat and protein you consume and decreases the amount of carbohydrates you eat. It is a high fat, high protein, and low carbs. Your daily caloric intake will follow the ratio of fat, protein, and carbs below (adjusting depending on your body type and health needs).

- 60 to 75 percent of fat calories
- 15 to 30 percent of protein calories
- 5 to 10 percent of carbs calories

How does the Keto Diet affect the body?

When you follow the keto diet, your body will enter a state of ketosis in approximately two to seven days. This is when there are not enough carbohydrates for your cells to burn for energy. In the next phase, your body will begin producing ketones, which will replace the burning of carbs for energy. The keto diet reprograms the body to use fat for energy, causing you to burn more fat in your body. After your body goes through ketosis and starts burning fat, you immediately lose water weight associated with eating carbs. Therefore, your initial weight loss can be quite significant. Over time, your body will naturally burn fat instead of carbs for energy.

What foods can I eat on the Keto Diet?

Trying a new diet usually means an overhaul in the way you think about putting together a meal, but you do not have to give up on filling flavorful foods. The keto diet is all about high fat and high protein, so you still indulge in some of your favorite foods just minus the hefty load of carbs. Foods high in fat such as avocados, nut butter, pistachios, and full-fat cheeses are staples in the keto diet. Instead of starchy high carb bases for dishes such as potatoes and rice, replace them with low carb options such as broccoli, cauliflower, and eggplant. The keto diet preaches high protein, so lean meats such as grass-fed bed, organic chicken, and fish such as salmon and tuna are essential to the diet. Also, if you think you have to give up snacking and dessert, you are wrong. The combination of low carb flours such as coconut and almond, with high-fat dairy such as almond milk, heavy cream, and Greek yogurt, can create a multitude of delicious desserts that rival the real thing! Ultimately, if your goal is to lose weight or just to have a more balanced diet to accompany a healthier lifestyle, then this diet will work for you! The recipes in this book prove you do not have to sacrifice flavor, texture, and cravings on the Keto Diet.

CHAPTER 1
BREAKFASTS

Start your day with a healthy,
energizing, and keto styled breakfast!

Mushroom and Goat Cheese Omelet

Total Prep & Cooking Time: 15. Min
Yields: 1 serving
Nutrition Facts: Calories: 489| Protein: 32g | Net Carbs: 8g | Fat: 37 g

Ingredients:
- 3 eggs
- 2 oz. crumbled goat cheese
- 2 tsp. half and half, milk or heavy cream
- 3 oz. mushrooms
- Pepper
- 2 tsp. olive oil
- Salt

Method:
1. Wash mushrooms and cut into thick and even slices.
2. Add olive oil to a heated skillet or pan, then toss in mushrooms and cook until lightly browned and soft – about four minutes.
3. While Mushrooms simmer, mix eggs with half and half (or milk or heavy cream), add seasonings, salt, and pepper and whisk together.
4. Crumble goat cheese and when mushroom finish, remove from skillet, and place on a cutting board.
5. Rinse out skillet before cooking omelet and reheat pan and add more olive oil before adding the egg mixture
6. When skillet heats up, add the eggs and cook until the outside edges are solidifying about 2 to 3 minutes.
7. Use a rubber spatula to check edges of eggs for firmness. Lift the omelet at a couple of places using the rubber spatula, then move the skillet around to cook the remaining eggs evenly.
8. Once the bottom of the egg is firmly cooked and the center still a little soft, add goat cheese and mushrooms.
9. Fold over the cooked omelet and roll onto the plate.

Mediterranean Omelet

Total Prep & Cooking Time: 20 min.
Yields: 2 servings
Nutrition Facts: Calories: 534| Protein: 33g | Net Carbs: 4g | Fat: 43g

Ingredients:
- 6 eggs
- 1 tsp. chopped fresh basil or dried basil
- 3 oz. cherry tomatoes
- 2 tsp. olive oil
- 5 oz. fresh mozzarella, diced or sliced
- Pepper and salt as desired
- Optional- Any other seasoning that you like on eggs

Method:
1. Preheat skillet and Cut cherry tomatoes in half.
2. Add olive oil to heated skillet or pan and cook tomatoes for 2 to 3 minutes.
3. While tomatoes are frying, add eggs to mixing bowl with any seasonings to taste and then beat briskly.
4. Pour beaten eggs in the skillet over and wait for the omelet to firm before adding in the sliced mozzarella.
5. Lower the heat and simmer until the omelet is firm.
6. Fold over the cooked and roll onto the plate.

Bacon and Brie Frittata

Total Prep & Cooking Time: 25 min.
Yields: 6 servings
Nutrition Facts: Calories: 338| Protein: 18g | Net Carbs: 1.8g | Fat: 27g

Ingredients:
- 8 large eggs
- ½ cup heavy whipping cream
- ½ tsp. salt
- 8 slices of bacon – chopped
- 2 cloves garlic minced
- 4 oz. thin sliced brie
- ½ tsp. pepper

Method:
1. Chop the bacon and thinly slice the brie – best to slice when it is cold.
2. Cook the bacon until crispy in an oven-ready 10-inch skillet. Then remove bacon and lay on plate to drain.
3. Leave behind the bacon grease and let the skillet cool down before proceeding.
4. Add eggs, cream, pepper, garlic, and salt, and whip. Then mix in about 2/3 of the bacon.
5. The skillet should be on medium heat and coat the entire skillet with the remaining bacon grease.
6. Add the mixed eggs into the skillet and let the eggs sit until the edges begin to loosen. Then layer the sliced brie on top of the eggs and add remaining bacon.
7. Turn broiler to high and position skillet on the rack. Broil for 2 to 5 minutes. Check and remove the eggs are bubbly and brown.
8. Once removed, allow the frittata to cool down for a couple of minutes before serving.

Baked Keto Breakfast Casserole

Total Prep & Cooking Time: 25 min.
Yields: 6-8 servings
Nutrition Facts: Calories: 392| Protein: 23.3g | Net Carbs: 5.9g | Fat: 30.5g

Ingredients:
- 6 eggs
- 16oz. spicy bulk sausage
- Salt
- 1 ½ cups Roma tomatoes
- 2 cups shredded mozzarella
- ½ cup heavy cream
- Pepper

Method:
1. Switch on the oven to 350 degrees. Dice tomatoes evenly.
2. Fry sausage while crumbling in the skillet and cook sausage fully.
3. Remove sausage from skillet and place into a 2-quart baking pan.
4. Layer diced tomatoes on top of sausage and then layer the cheese.
5. Lastly, add heavy cream to eggs and blend.
6. Transfer eggs over the casserole.
7. Bake for 30-40 minutes until cheese is bubbling.
8. Let it cool and set for 15 minutes after removing from the oven.

Bacon and Egg Breakfast Cups

Total Prep & Cooking Time: 35 min.
Yields: 12 servings
Nutrition Facts: Calories: 174| Protein: 13.3g | Net Carbs: 0.7g | Fat: 12.9g

Ingredients

12 large eggs
Pepper
12 pieces of bacon
Salt
1 tbsp. chopped chives

Method:
1. Switch on the oven to 400 degrees.
2. Cook bacon for 8-10 minutes, until it is soft but not crispy. Remove the bacon and place on paper towels to drain.
3. Smear the muffin pan with oil or butter.
4. Place one piece of bacon in each cup, wrapping it around the sides. Crack one egg into the cup. Sprinkle the casserole with chives, pepper, and salt as desired.
5. Cook for 12-15 minutes so that the bacon is crispy. Monitor closely.

Eggs Benedict Avocado Bowl

Total Prep & Cooking Time: 15 min.
Yields:4 servings
Nutrition Facts: Calories: 567| Protein: 16.2g | Net Carbs: 9.6g | Fat: 53.4g

Ingredients:

Hollandaise:
- 3 egg yolks
- 8 ½ tbsp. butter, unsalted
- Pepper and salt as desired
- 1 tbsp. lemon juice

Eggs Benedict:
- 2 avocados, peal and pitted
- 4 eggs
- 5 oz. smoked salmon

Method:
1. Melt the butter in a microwave-safe container for about 20 seconds.
2. Split the yellow yolks from the egg whites. Join egg yolks and lemon juice into the butter and blend until you form a creamy white layer. Then slowly blend, lifting, and lowering to create a creamy sauce.
3. Boil water in a small saucepan and then reduce the boiling pot of water to a medium to low heat.
4. Then crack each egg into a small bowl or measuring cup. Then slowly put each egg into the water.
5. Stir the water in a circle, creating a small vortex to prevent the egg white from separating from the yolk—Cook for 3-4 minutes, or until the yolk is at your preferred consistency. Remove poached eggs - slotted spoons work best and lay tenderly on a paper towel-lined dish to absorb extra water.
6. Cut avocados in half, peel the skin and remove the pit. Then slice avocado evenly so it will be sturdy on the plate.
7. Place each poached egg on each half of the avocado and add a scoop of hollandaise sauce. Eat the smoked salmon on the side or top of the eggs.
8. Eat immediately.

Tex-Mex Scrambled Eggs

Total Prep & Cooking Time: 15 min.
Yields:4 servings
Nutrition Facts: Calories: 240| Protein: 13.9g | Net Carbs: 2.7g | Fat: 19.4g

Ingredients:
- 6 oz. eggs
- 1 tomato, diced
- 1 oz. butter
- 1 scallion, finely chopped
- 2 pickled jalapenos, thinly chopped
- 3 oz. cheese, shredded
- Pepper and salt as desired

Method:
1. Chop the scallions, tomatoes, and jalapenos, or to the desired size.
2. Melt a portion of butter. Next fry the scallions, jalapenos, and tomatoes for 3-4 minutes.
3. Whisk eggs and then transfer into frying pan and scramble for about 2 minutes.
4. Add cheese, and spices as desired as toppings.

Cauliflower Hash Browns

Total Prep & Cooking Time: 40 min.
Yields: 4 servings
Nutrition Facts: Calories: 284| Protein: 6.8g | Net Carbs: 7.6g | Fat: 26.4g

Ingredients:

- 1 lb. cauliflower
- 3 eggs
- ½ yellow onion, grated
- 1 tsp. salt
- 2 pinches pepper
- 4 oz. butter for frying

Method:

1. Clean and grate the cauliflower and onion using a grater or food processor.
2. Mix cauliflower and other ingredients. Let sit for about 5-10 minutes.
3. Melt enough butter or oil for frying in a large skillet over medium heat. You should be able to fit about 3-4 hash browns about 3-4 inches wide at a time.
4. Scoop grated cauliflower
5. Tip- place the first batch in oven on low heat to keep warm
6. Scoop grated cauliflower into the heated skillet and flatten them to be about 3-4 inches wide.
7. Fry hash browns for about 4-5 minutes on each side – watching closely, so they do not burn but do not flip hash browns too soon, or they may fall apart.

Coconut Pancakes

Total Prep & Cooking Time: 40 min.
Yields: 4 servings
Nutrition Facts: Calories: 299| Protein: 11.3g | Net Carbs: 11.6g | Fat: 23.8g

Ingredients:
- 6 eggs
- ¾ cup coconut milk
- Salt
- 2 tbsp. melted coconut oil
- 1 tsp. baking powder
- ½ cup coconut flour
- Coconut oil or Butter

Method:
1. Divide the egg whites from the yellow yolks. Then thrash the egg whites with a smidgen of salt with a hand mixer. Whip eggs until stiff peaks form and then set off to the side.
2. In another bowl, whisk coconut oil, coconut milk, and egg yolks together. Then add baking powder and coconut flour and unite into a batter.
3. Carefully add the egg whites into the smooth batter, and the batter should rest for 5 minutes.
4. Heat skillet over medium heat. Make even scoops and fry pancakes in coconut oil or butter for a few minutes on each side. Gently flip pancakes.
5. Serve with your favorite pancake toppings.

Keto English Muffins

Total Prep & Cooking Time: 15 min.
Yields: 4 servings
Nutrition Facts: Calories: 185| Protein: 5.1g | Net Carbs: 6g | Fat: 15.8g

Ingredients:
- 2 tbsp. coconut flour
- 2 eggs
- Salt
- Coconut oil or Butter for frying
- ½ tsp. baking powder

Method:
1. Mix the dry ingridents in a standard mixing bowl.
2. Then fuse with eggs and whisk all ingredients together. Let sit for a couple of minutes.
3. Add melted butter to a frying pan over medium heat and place 3 scoops of batter into pan.
4. Flip the muffins after a couple minutes and continue frying.
5. Then let cool and serve with your favorite toppings.

Keto Oatmeal

Total Prep & Cooking Time: 10 min.
Yields: 4 servings
Nutrition Facts: Calories: 592| Protein: 31g | Net Carbs: 4g | Fat: 47g

Ingredients:
- ¼ cup hulled hem seeds
- 1 tbsp. Vital Proteins Collagen Peptides
- ½ tbsp. chia seeds
- ½ coconut milk or heavy cream
- 1 tbsp. golden flaxseed meal
- Optional: keto-approved sweetener such as erythritol, salt, or your favorite oatmeal add-ins.

Method:
1. Mix the hemp seeds, flax seeds, vital proteins collagen, and chia seeds in a small saucepan. Also, add optional sweeteners, salt, or oatmeal add-ins.
2. Then stir in cream or milk and mix until smooth.
3. Let simmer for a couple minutes until oatmeal starts to thicken.
4. Serve immediately and add additional toppings if wanted.

Keto Whipped Coffee

Total Prep & Cooking Time: 15 min.
Yields: 2 servings
Nutrition Facts: Calories: 117| Protein: 2.8g | Net Carbs: 47g | Fat: 9.6g

Ingredients:
- 1 1/w tbsp. espresso instant coffee powder
- 1 ½ tbsp. erythritol or sugar substitute
- 2 tbsp. hot, or boiled water
- 1 tsp. vanilla extract (optional)
- 1 ½ cups unsweetened almond milk or coconut milk
- Ice cubes, for serving

Method:
1. To make the whipped topping, you can use a whisk, handheld frother, or an immersion blender (which is the fastest method).
2. Mix the espresso powder, erythritol, and hot water in a glass jar or drinking glass.
3. Blend the mixture in the glass with an immersion blender over high speed or whisk or about 3 minutes. As the coffee mixture blends, it will go from dark to light brown and become whipped cream.
4. In a separate glass, fill with ice about 2/3 full and pour in almond milk, vanilla extract, and stir.
5. Top with whipped coffee and mix.

Strawberry and Avocado Smoothie

Total Prep & Cooking Time: 5 min.
Yields: 1 serving
Nutrition Facts: Calories: 106| Protein: 1g | Net Carbs: 12g | Fat: 7g

Ingredients:
- 1 lb. frozen strawberries
- 1 ½ cups almond milk
- 1 large avocado
- ¼ powdered allulose or substitute sweetener

Method:
1. Put all the ingredients into the blender and mix until desired consistency.
2. Add sweetener to taste.
3. Add less liquid to make it thicker and more milk to make it thinner.

CHAPTER 2 MEALS

Filling meals packed with protein and fat.

Balsamic Chicken Tenders

Total Prep & Cooking Time: 20 min.
Yields: 4 servings
Nutrition Facts: Calories: 311 | Protein: 48g | Net Carbs: 4g | Fat 9g

Ingredients:
- 2 lbs. chicken tenders or chicken breast
- 1 tsp. salt
- 1/3 balsamic vinegar
- 2 sundried tomato halves, sliced
- 1 tsp. olive oil
- 8 basil leaves – chopped
- ½ pepper

Method:
1. Heat a big skillet and grease with olive oil and stick the tenders in the oil and dash with salt and pepper.
2. Cook each tender for about 4 minutes or until they are cooked on each side and all the way through.
3. Transfer the chicken from the frying pan and decrease the heat to medium. Then toss in balsamic vinegar and sundried tomatoes.
4. Cook down the tomatoes and balsamic vinegar by half and then add the chicken back to the frying pan.
5. Coat chicken with balsamic glaze and then transfer to a plate. Garnish with chopped basil.

Broiled Chicken with Artichokes

Total Prep & Cooking Time: 30 min.
Yields: 4 servings
Nutrition Facts: Calories: 261 | Protein: 33g | Net Carbs: 5g | Fat 10

Ingredients:

- 2 tbsp. minced garlic
- 1 ½ lbs. boneless skinless chicken thighs
- Pepper and salt as desired
- 1-2 jars of artichokes hearts (10 oz. jars)
- 2 tbsp. oregano

Method:

1. In a large bowl, mix chicken thighs and artichokes hearts (including liquid) and let it marinate for about 20-30 minutes.
2. After chicken marinates, strain the liquid and toss in remaining spices and garlic. Combine all ingredients.
3. Set broiler on the oven to high and put marinated chicken in for about 18 -25 minutes, so chicken thoroughly cooks.
4. Broil on the second rack for about 18-20 minutes, then broil on the first rack for the last 5 minutes to make chicken a little crispy.

Roasted Paprika Chicken and Rutabaga

Total Prep & Cooking Time: 55 min.
Yields: 4 servings
Nutrition Facts: Calories: 857| Protein: 69g | Net Carbs: 34g | Fat 49g

Ingredients:

- 2 lbs. chicken thighs or drumsticks
- ¼ cup olive oil
- 2 lbs. rutabaga, cut and peeled
- 1 tbsp. paprika
- Pepper and salt as desired

Paprika and Garlic Mayo:

- Pepper and salt as desired
- 1 tsp. paprika
- 1 cup mayonnaise
- 1 tsp. garlic powder

Method:

1. Preheat oven to 400 degrees and chop the rutabaga in 2-3 inch pieces
2. Place the chicken and rutabaga in a baking dish and generously toss in seasonings. Then add olive oil and mix all ingredients.
3. Bake the chicken for about 40 minutes or until cook all the way through. Monitor closely and lower the heat if chicken or rutabaga starts to get too brown.
4. Mix all the seasonings with the mayo and serve with chicken and rutabaga.

Keto Fried Chicken with Broccoli

Total Prep & Cooking Time: 35 min.
Yields: 4 servings
Nutrition Facts: Calories: 625 | Protein: 53g | Net Carbs: 9.6g | Fat 41.8g

Ingredients:
- 1 ½ lbs. boneless chicken thighs
- 5 oz. butter
- 1lb. broccoli
- ½ leek
- 1 tsp. garlic powder

Method:
1. Over medium heat, add half of the butter.
2. Generously coat the chicken with spices and then lay into a heated frying pan.
3. Flip the chicken until it is cook thoroughly and browned on both sides. Cook for about 20-25 minutes – adjust time according to the size of chicken thighs.
4. Remove chicken from the pan and keep them warm in foil on low heat in the oven.
5. While chicken is frying, rinse and chop the broccoli, including the stem into small pieces. Then clean the leeks thoroughly and cut the leeks into pieces.
6. Using a different skillet, dissolve the butter over middle heat and add all of the spices or seasonings. Next, put in the leeks, so they soften and then add the broccoli, stirring occasionally. Cook vegetables until tender.
7. Plate the chicken and vegetables and serve with extra melted butter on top.

Chicken Pesto Zoodle Salad

Total Prep & Cooking Time: 25 min.
Yields: 4 servings
Nutrition Facts: Calories: 589| Protein: 43.8g | Net Carbs: 9.5g | Fat 42g

Ingredients:

- 1 lb. chicken breasts
- 5 oz. cherry tomatoes, cut in half
- 8 oz. sugar-free green pesto
- 4 oz. feta cheese, crumbled or cubed
- 14 oz. zucchini, 2 medium or store-bought zucchini noodles
- 1 tbsp. olive oil

Method:

1. Position the chicken in a standard pot and overlay with cold water.
2. Increase heat to boil and then decrease to medium to low heat to let the chicken simmer for 15 minutes or until cooked all the way through.
3. Transfer the chicken from the water, set aside to cool down for a few minutes, and then shred.
4. For medium zucchini, use a spiralizer and then place zoodles in the mixing bowl.
5. In a large mixing bowl, pour pesto over zoodles and toss, completely coating the zoodles. Then add shredded chicken feta and tomatoes into the bowl.
6. Toss all the salad ingredients and then drizzle with olive oil

Turkey Taco Casserole

Total Prep & Cooking Time: 45 min.
Yields: 6 servings
Nutrition Facts: Calories: 367| Protein: 45g | Net Carbs: 6g | Fat 18g

Ingredients:
- 8 oz. shredded cheese
- 1 ½ - 2 lbs. ground turkey
- 1 cup salsa
- 2 tbsp. taco seasoning
- 16 oz. cottage cheese

Method:
1. Switch on the oven to 400 degrees.
2. In a sizeable casserole dish, put in the ground meat and mix in the taco seasoning—Bake for 20 minutes.
3. While ground turkey is baking, mix 1 cup of shredded cheese, cottage cheese, and salsa.
4. Take the casserole from the oven and strain out any leftover juices from the ground meat.
5. Pound and crush the meat into smaller pieces and then layer the cottage cheese and salsa combo over the meat. Sprinkle remaining cheese on top of the ground meat.
6. Put the casserole back into the oven and bake for 15-20 minutes until the meat cooks all the way through. And the cheese is melted and bubbling.

Turkey Breasts with Cream Cheese Sauce

Total Prep & Cooking Time: 25 min.
Yields: 4 servings
Nutrition Facts: Calories: 619| Protein: 35.3g | Net Carbs: 12.4g | Fat 48.4g

Ingredients:
- 1 ½ lbs. turkey breast
- 2 cups heavy whipping cream
- 7 oz. cream cheese
- 1 tbsp. soy sauce
- 1 ½ oz. small capers
- 2 tbsp. butter
- Pepper and salt as desired

Method:
1. Switch on the oven to 375 degrees.
2. In a sizeable oven-safe skillet, dissolve 1 tablespoon the butter over moderate heat. Then flavor the turkey with desired spices.
3. Fry turkey breast until golden brown on each side.
4. Finish baking the turkey breast in the oven until the turkey cooks through. Then place on plate and cover with foil.
5. Pour remaining turkey drippings into a small saucepan. Combine the heavy whipping cream with the cream cheese. Bring the cream to a soft boil and stir.
6. Decrease the heat and allow the sauce simmer until it thickens. Then add the soy sauce and a dash of salt and pepper.
7. Melt remaining butter in the skillet and sauté the capers until they are crispy.
8. Pour sauce over turkey breasts and garnish with capers.

Turkey Sausage and Kale Soup

Total Prep & Cooking Time: 20 min.
Yields: 6 servings
Nutrition Facts: Calories: 164| Protein: 20g | Net Carbs: 9g | Fat 3g

Ingredients:

- 1 lb. Italian turkey sausage
- ½ cup onion, diced
- 15 oz. tomatoes, diced
- 32 oz. chicken broth
- 8 oz. Kale, chopped
- Pepper and salt as desired

Method:

1. if not already pre-cut, dice the onion and tomatoes. Take sausage out of the casing, if necessary, and cut into small pieces. Chop kale and remove the stem.
2. Turn on pressure cooker on low to brown the sausage. Then once sausage browns, add chicken broth, diced onions, and tomatoes to the pressure cooker.
3. Close the lid and shut the steam valve. Set pressure to high and leave for 15 minutes.
4. While soup starts to cook, add chopped kale and ½ cup of water in a microwave-safe dish. Cover the dish and heat up for 3-4 minutes or until kale is tender. Then drain water from the kale dish and set aside.
5. When pressure cooker finishes, open the steam valve and let the steam release for about 10 minutes.
6. Add kale before serving.

No Noodle Keto Lasagna

Total Prep & Cooking Time: 40 min.
Yields: 8 servings
Nutrition Facts: Calories: 355 | Protein: 24g | Net Carbs: 6g | Fat 25g

Ingredients:
- 1 lb. ground beef
- 1 ½ cups ricotta cheese, whole milk
- 25 oz. Marinara sauce
- 8 oz. sliced mozzarella cheese
- Pepper and salt as desired
- ½ cup parmesan cheese, grated

Method:
1. Turn oven to 350 degrees.
2. Add salt and pepper to ground beef.
3. Then heat a big skillet over medium and toss in the ground beef. Then prepare the meat, mixing and breaking meat until browned. Drain any excess liquid.
4. Add beef to 9x9 inch baking pan.
5. Layer the ricotta and then parmesan on top of the ground meat. Then pour marinara sauce over layers of cheese. Sprinkle mozzarella cheese on top.
6. Bake the no noodle lasagna for 25 minutes. Do not take out unless cheese is golden brown and melted.

Keto Stuffed Cheese Meatloaf

Total Prep & Cooking Time: 65 min.
Yields: 6 servings
Nutrition Facts: Calories: 183| Protein: 11g | Net Carbs: 3g | Fat 18g

Ingredients:
- 1 lb. ground beef
- 2 eggs
- 1 tbsp. dried marjoram
- 2 buffalo mozzarellas
- Pepper and salt as desired
- 2 whole leeks

Method:
1. Turn on oven to 365 degrees.
2. Totally scrub the leaks clean and cut about ½ from the white part. Cut the white part into small pieces. Separate the rest of the leek into single leaves.
3. Boil a big pot of water and place the leaves inside the boiling water for about 3-4 minutes. Then withdraw leaves from pot and rinse in cold water. Set leeks aside to dry.
4. In a large bowl, add ground beef, cut white leek ends, marjoram, eggs, salt, and pepper.
5. In a baking dish or a loaf pan, arrange the leek leaves on the bottom with sides leaning over. Then fill the bottom and side with the ground meat mixture.
6. Add mozzarella inside and finish with another layer of ground meat.
7. Then cover the dish with leek ends and add more leaves if needed.
8. Put in the keto meatloaf and bake for 50 minutes. Bake the first 40 minutes covered with foil and the last 10 minutes uncovered.

Mozzarella -Spinach Stuffed Burgers

Total Prep & Cooking Time: 25 min.
Yields: 4 servings
Nutrition Facts: Calories: 414| Protein: 36g | Net Carbs: 1g | Fat 29g

Ingredients:
- 1 ½ lbs. ground chuck
- 2 tbsp. parmesan, grated
- 2 cups fresh spinach
- ½ cup shredded mozzarella cheese
- Pepper and salt as desired

Method:
1. In a standard mixing bowl, join ground chuck and season accordingly. Then scoop about 1/3 cup of meat mixture and shape into 8 patties about ½ inch thick. Set in refrigerator.
2. Cook spinach over medium heat for a couple minutes until the spinach wilts. Drain spinach and let it cool before squeezing out excess liquid.
3. Move spinach to cutting board and chop the spinach. Add spinach, mozzarella cheese, and parmesan to a separate mixing bowl. Stir all ingredients together.
4. Take beef patties out of the fridge and scoop about ¼ cup of stuffing and place in the center of 4 patties.
5. Cover with remaining beef patties and press edges together firmly to seal the stuffing inside the patties. Round out the edges of the patties to create a single thick patty.
6. Heat a pan or grill to medium-high and prepare stuffed burgers for 5 to 6 minutes on, grilling equally on each side.

Slow Cooker Moroccan Beef

Total Prep & Cooking Time: 10hrs.
Yields: 8 servings
Nutrition Facts: Calories: 414| Protein: 36g | Net Carbs: 1g | Fat 29g

Ingredients:
- 2 lbs. beef roast
- ½ cup sliced yellow onions
- Pepper and salt as desired
- 4 tbsp. garam masala seasoning

Method:
1. First, slice the onion into thin strips and place them into the slow cooker.
2. Place the beef roast into the slow cooker on top of the onions and then add seasonings.
3. Cook on low heat in the crockpot for 8 hours, then shred beef with a fork and then cook on the lowest settings for another 2 hours letting the spices marinate the beef.

Steak with Garlic Butter Mushrooms

Total Prep & Cooking Time: 25 mins.
Yields: 4 servings
Nutrition Facts: Calories: 292| Protein: 36g | Net Carbs: 1g | Fat 29g

Ingredients:

Steak:
- 1 lb. grass-fed top sirloin steak
- 4 tsp. ghee, room temperature
- 1 tsp. fresh garlic
- Salt to taste

Mushrooms:
- 2 cups white mushrooms
- Salt
- 2 tsp. ghee, melted
- 1 tsp. fresh garlic

Method:

1. Mince the garlic for the steak and mushrooms and set to the side.
2. Preheat the grill and set it to high heat. Pat dry the steak and, in a bowl, combine the garlic and ghee. Then cover one side of the steak with mixture and season with pepper and salt as desired.
3. Once the grill is heated, place the ghee and garlic side of the steak, cook for 4-5 minutes, or until the steak is charred. Then add the remaining ghee and garlic mixture on the steak and flip to cook until desired doneness. Remove from heat.
4. In a separate bowl, combine mushrooms with melted ghee, garlic, salt, and pepper. Wrap mushrooms in 2 layers of tin foil, shiny side inward, and put mushrooms in the center to create a tight packet.
5. Cook mushrooms on the grill for 5 minutes and then flip and grill until mushrooms are tender.
6. Serve steak topped with mushrooms.

Philly Cheesesteak Stuffed Peppers

Total Prep & Cooking Time: 5o min.
Yields: 8 servings
Nutrition Facts: Calories: 251 | Protein: 19g | Net Carbs: 5g | Fat 17g

Ingredients:
- 4 green peppers
- 1 cup yellow onion, diced
- 1 lb. steak, sliced thin
- Pepper and salt as desired
- 1 tbsp. olive oil
- 8 slices provolone cheese

Method:
1. Turn0020soven to 400 degrees. Thinly slice steak and chop the yellow onion.
2. Slice all green peppers in half and remove seeds and white center. Put peppers in casserole dip, cut side up, and add about ¼ inch of water. Cover with foil and then put the dish in the oven.
3. In a frying pan, heat olive oil and toss in diced onions, cooking until translucent.
4. Place steak into the frying pan with onions. Then cook for 5 minutes or until preferred doneness. Add pepper and salt as desired.
5. Take peppers out of the oven and add a dash of salt and pepper to each half. Then stuff each pepper with steak and onion mixture.
6. Layer one slice of provolone cheese on top of each pepper and put back. Leave exposed and cook for about 20 minutes.

Pork Chops with Caramelized Onions and Bacon

Total Prep & Cooking Time: 5o min.
Yields: 4 servings
Nutrition Facts: Calories: 451 | Protein: 29.6g | Net Carbs: 3.4g | Fat 34.7g

Ingredients:
- 4 oz. bacon, chopped
- 1 yellow onion, thinly sliced
- 4 pork chops
- ½ cup chicken broth
- ¼ cup heavy whipping cream

Method:
1. Fry bacon over medium heat or until preferred crispiness. Use a slotted spatula or spoon to remove bacon and leave bacon grease in skillet.
2. Add onion, salt, and pepper to bacon grease. Continuously rotate the onions and cook for about 15 to 20 minutes until onions are golden brown and soft.
3. Add onions in the same bowl as the bacon. Generously season pork chops with pepper and salt.
4. Increase the heat on the stove to moderate and arrange the seasoned pork chops to the skillet. Brown the first side of the pork chops for about 3 minutes and then flip.
5. Reduce heat to medium and continue cooking pork chops for another 7 to 10 minutes or until pork chops are cooked through. Then remove chops to plate.
6. Add broth to skillet and scrape any bits left. Then add heavy cream and simmer until the mixture thickens. Put bacon and onions back to the skillet and stir to combine all ingredients.
7. Serve pork chops with bacon and onion mixture on top.

Pork and Green Pepper Keto Stir-Fry

Total Prep & Cooking Time: 20 min.
Yields: 2 servings
Nutrition Facts: Calories: 676| Protein: 40g | Net Carbs: 14.2g | Fat 51.7g

Ingredients:
- 2/3 lb. pork shoulder
- 2 green bell peppers
- 2 scallions, sliced
- 1 tsp. chili paste
- 1 oz. almond
- Pepper and salt as desired
- 4 oz. butter for cooking

Method:
1. Melt a portion butter in a frying pan or wok. Save some butter for serving. Slice the green peppers and scallions and set aside—also, pre-cut pork shoulder into strips.
2. Add pork to the frying pan and prepare the meat over very high heat for a couple minutes.
3. Throw the vegetables and chili paste into the pan and keep stirring vegetables for another couple of minutes—season with pepper and salt as desired.
4. Plate in a nice serving dish and top with almonds and room temperature butter.

Bacon-Wrapped Pork Chops

Total Prep & Cooking Time: 40 min.
Yields: 6-8 servings
Nutrition Facts: Calories: 513| Protein: 51g | Net Carbs: 1g | Fat 34g

Ingredients:
- 12 oz. bacon package
- 6 to 8 boneless pork chops
- Pepper and salt as desired

Method:
1. Line cooking sheet with wax paper. Turn oven to 350 degrees.
2. Use a cutting board or a plate, season pork chops with pepper and salt as desired.
3. Open bacon and completely wrap each pork chop. Then place the pork chops on a lined baking sheet.
4. Sprinkle more salt and pepper over the bacon-wrapped pork chops.
5. Bake for 30 minutes and flip after the first 15 minutes. Make sure to cook the pork chops all the way through.

Crispy Bacon and Fried Cabbage

Total Prep & Cooking Time: 20 min.
Yields: 2 servings
Nutrition Facts: Calories: 774| Protein: 38.3g | Net Carbs: 14.6g | Fat 62.2g

Ingredients:
- 10 oz. bacon package
- 2 oz. butter
- 1 lb. green cabbage
- Pepper and salt as desired

Method:
1. Slice the bacon and cabbage into small pieces.
2. In a sizeable skillet over the moderate heat, fry the bacon until crispy.
3. Add butter and cabbage to the skillet and brown the cabbage. Dash with pepper and salt as desired.

Fried Salmon with Broccoli and Lemon Mayo

Total Prep & Cooking Time: 25 min.
Yields: 4 servings
Nutrition Facts: Calories: 634| Protein: 42.4g | Net Carbs: 21.7g | Fat 43.8g

Ingredients:

Salmon and Broccoli:
- 1 ¾ lbs. salmon
- 1 lb. broccoli
- 2 oz. butter
- Pepper and salt as desired

Lemon Mayo:
- 1 cup mayonnaise
- 2 tbsp. lemon juice

Method:
1. Rinse and chop the broccoli, including the stem, in bite-sized pieces.
2. Then mix the lemon juice and mayo and let sit.
3. Spice up the salmon with pepper and salt as desired and divide salmon in serving-sized portions.
4. Add about half the butter to the frying pan and grill the salmon over moderate heat for a few minutes. Lessen the heat and cook each side evenly. Take out from the pan and enclose in foil to keep the salmon warm.
5. Using the same skillet, add the other half of the butter and cook down the broccoli for 3-4 minutes over medium heat until the broccoli is tender but not mushy. Add pepper and salt as desired.
6. Serve the salmon and broccoli with lemon mayo on the side.

Pistachio Crusted Salmon

Total Prep & Cooking Time: 25 min.
Yields: 4 servings
Nutrition Facts: Calories: 269| Protein: 23g | Net Carbs: 6g | Fat 17g

Ingredients:

- 1 lb. salmon or 1 large filet
- ¼ cup parmesan cheese, grated
- 1/3 cup pistachios, crushed or chopped
- Pepper and salt as desired
- ¼ panko breadcrumbs

Method:

1. Switch oven to 400 degrees. Crush or finely chop the pistachios if necessary.
2. Mix the pistachios, breadcrumbs, and cheese in a bowl.
3. Arrange foil to a sizeable pan and smear the foil with oil. Then place salmon on greased foil, skin side down. Sprinkle pepper and salt as desired.
4. Top the salmon with pistachio mixture, pressing firmly, so the mixture adheres.
5. Then bake with the pan exposed for 15-20 minutes, or until the seasoned salmon easily flakes.

Spanish Garlic Shrimp

Total Prep & Cooking Time: 35 min.
Yields: 4 servings
Nutrition Facts: Calories: 355| Protein: 31.6g | Net Carbs: 15g | Fat 19.2g

Ingredients:
- 18 oz. shrimp, peeled with tail on
- 1 ½ oz. garlic cloves
- 1 tsp. chili flakes
- 3 tbsp. fresh parsley
- 1 lemon cut into wedges

Method:
1. Peel shrimp and leave the tail on. Chop and peel garlic cloves. Mince the fresh parsley. Cut lemon into wedges.
2. Use a large cast-iron skillet and warm oil over moderate heat.
3. Toss the garlic and chili flakes into the skillet, and then cover for 5 minutes or until garlic turns light yellow. Stir occasionally to cook evenly.
4. While garlic is cooking, season the shrimp with salt and set aside for five minutes.
5. When the garlic turns light yellow, raise the heat and toss in the shrimp. Stir and space the shrimp evenly, with no overlapping. Cook shrimp until bright pink and flip to cook evenly on both sides.
6. Remove shrimp from heat and garnish with parsley and lemon wedges to serve.

Keto Pizza

Total Prep & Cooking Time: 30 min.
Yields: 4 servings
Nutrition Facts: Calories: 679| Protein: 60.3g | Net Carbs: 7.9g | Fat 45.7g

Ingredients:

Crust:
- 4 eggs
- 6oz. shredded mozzarella

Topping:
- 3 tbsp. unsweetened tomato sauce
- 1 tsp. dried oregano
- 5 oz. shredded mozzarella
- 1 ½ oz. pepperoni

Method:
1. Switch oven to 400 degrees
2. First, to prepare the crust, use a medium bowl to combine eggs and shredded cheese. Stir thoroughly to combine.
3. Spread the egg and cheese dough on a parchment paper on a big baking sheet.
4. Use the dough to form 2 circular pizzas or 1 big rectangular pizza. Bake for 15 minutes or until pizza crust is crispy at edges and semi-soft and golden brown in the center. Pull out the crust and let sit for a couple minutes.
5. Turn up the heat on the oven to 450 degrees. Then spread tomato sauce on crust and then dash oregano on top of sauce. Lastly, add the cheese and arrange the pepperoni on top of cheese.
6. Bake pizza for 5-10 more minutes until toppings are bubbling and golden.

Broccoli and Cheese Soup

Total Prep & Cooking Time: 20 min.
Yields: 4 servings
Nutrition Facts: Calories: 292| Protein: 60.3g | Net Carbs: 7.9g | Fat 45.7g

Ingredients:
- 1 cup heavy cream
- 4 cups of broccoli – florets
- 4 cloves of garlic
- 3 ½ cups of vegetable broth
- 3 cups cheddar cheese, shredded

Method:
1. Cut the broccoli into florets and mince the garlic. Sauté the garlic over medium heat in a large pot for 1 minute or until garlic is fragrant.
2. Combine the vegetable broth, chopped broccoli, and heavy cream in the pot. Boil first and then decrease to simmer for 10 -20 minutes. Check that the vegetables are soft.
3. Remove about 1/3 broccoli and set aside.
4. Then insert the immersion blender into the pot and puree all the ingredients together.
5. Reduce the heat and add the shredded cheddar cheese about ½ cup at a time. Repeatedly swirl until the cheese is melted. Then puree the soup again to make a smooth consistency.
6. Remove from heat and garnish with remaining broccoli florets.

Zucchini Soup

Total Prep & Cooking Time: 30 min.
Yields: 4 servings
Nutrition Facts: Calories: 292| Protein: 60.3g | Net Carbs: 7.9g | Fat 45.7g

Ingredients:

- ¼ cup heavy cream
- 16 oz. chicken broth
- 7 oz. onion, sliced
- 2 cloves garlic
- 28 oz. zucchini, sliced
- Pepper and salt as desired

Method:

1. Pre-cut the zucchini and onion into slices.
2. Add sliced onion and zucchini, garlic and broth to a large pot. Boil and then decrease to moderate heat and let the soup simmer for about 20 minutes. Keep stirring.
3. Remove pot from heat once the zucchini is soft and insert an immersion blender to puree the soup.
4. Keep blending until smooth. Add in heavy cream, salt, and pepper and stir thoroughly.

CHAPTER 3
SNACKS & APPETIZERS

Yummy snacks and appetizers that satisfy
any cravings and keep your diet on track.

Broccoli Cheddar Loaf

Total Prep & Cooking Time: 35 min.
Yields: 10 servings
Nutrition Facts: Calories: 90 Protein: 6g | Net Carbs: 2g | Fat 6g

Ingredients:

- 5 eggs
- ¾ cup raw broccoli florets
- 2 tsp. baking powder
- 1 cup shredded cheddar cheese
- 3 ½ tbsp coconut flour
- 1 tsp. salt

Method:

1. Chop the broccoli florets into smaller pieces.
2. Preheat oven to 350 degrees. Use cooking spray to oil the pan.
3. Combine all the ingredients and transfer to the loaf pan.
4. Bake for 30-35 minutes, so the bread is lightly toasted on top and puffy.

Keto Bread

Total Prep & Cooking Time: 70 min.
Yields: 1 serving
Nutrition Facts: Calories: 450 Protein: 19g | Net Carbs: 10g | Fat 40g

Ingredients:
- 1 ½ cup finely ground almond flour
- ¼ cups of butter, melted
- ½ tsp. salt
- 6 eggs
- 1 tbsp. baking powder

Method:
1. Switch on the oven to 375 degrees. Position wax paper in a loaf pan (8" by 4"). Then separate egg whites and yolks.
2. Join egg whites with cream of tartar in a standard bowl and then use a hand mixer to whip until peaks form.
3. In a different bowl, use a hand mixer to combine egg yolks, almond flour, melted butter, baking powder, and salt.
4. Fold in about 1/3 of the whipped egg whites and then transfer the rest of the egg whites. Continue to fold.
5. Pour the well-mixed batter into the loaf pan, smoothing out as you pour.
6. Bake for 30 minutes. Let the bread cool for about 30 minutes before slicing.

Meaty Pizza Cups

Total Prep & Cooking Time: 25 min.
Yields: 1 serving
Nutrition Facts: Calories: 450 Protein: 19g | Net Carbs: 10g | Fat 40g

Ingredients:
- 24 Pepperoni pieces
- 12 thin-sliced deli ham
- 12 tbsp. pizza sauce, sugar-free
- 1 lb. Italian sausage, sugar-free
- 3 cups Mozzarella cheese

Method:
1. Switch on the oven to 375 degrees and then brown the Italian sausage in a skillet. Drain the excess grease from the pan.
2. Line the muffin tins with deli ham and evenly divvy up the sausage and the balance of the ingredients into each cup.
3. Bake for 10 minutes. Then switch oven to broil for 1 minute until edges of the meat are crispy and cheese is bubbly.
4. Shift the meaty cups from each muffin tin and set on a paper toweled lined plate. Eat immediately or refrigerate.

Keto Chicken Nuggets

Total Prep & Cooking Time: 20 min.
Yields: 6 servings
Nutrition Facts: Calories: 243 Protein: 18g | Net Carbs: 2g | Fat 17g

Ingredients:
- 2 cups cooked chicken
- 1 tsp garlic salt
- 8 oz. cream cheese
- 1 egg
- ¼ almond flour

Method:
1. Preheat oven to 350 degrees.
2. Cook 2 cups of chicken and then shred it with an electric mixer. Use a combination of white meat and dark meat. The chicken should be slightly warm when shredded.
3. Combine the shredded chicken with the rest of the ingredients and mix thoroughly.
4. Put scoops of chicken mixture on a greased baking sheet or parchment-lined baking sheet. Flatten each scoop into a nugget shape.
5. Bake nuggets for 12-14 minutes. So, when you take nuggets out of the oven, they are golden brown.

Slow Cooker Buffalo Chicken

Total Prep & Cooking Time: 20 min.
Yields: 6 servings
Nutrition Facts: Calories: 147| Protein: 23g | Net Carbs: 6g | Fat 3g

Ingredients:

- 2 tbsp. ranch salad dressing mix
- ½ cup Buffalo wing sauce
- 4 boneless skinless chicken breasts
- Optional: celery and crumbled blue cheese

Method:

1. Using a 3-quart slow cooker, combine the wing sauce, ranch dressing mix, and chicken. Cover the slow cooker and simmer on low for 3-4 hours or until meat is totally tender.
2. Once chicken is cooked, shred with 2 forks. You can serve on celery or top with additional wing sauce and blue cheese.

Rosemary Garlic Chicken Kabobs

Total Prep & Cooking Time: 30 min.
Yields: 8 servings
Nutrition Facts: Calories: 110| Protein: 9g | Net Carbs: 1g | Fat 8g

Ingredients:
- 3 boneless skinless chicken breasts
- 8 bamboo skewers
- ¼ cup olive oil
- 2 tbsp. fresh rosemary, chopped
- 3 cloves of garlic
- Pepper and salt as desired

Method:
1. Saturate bamboo skewers in water for 15 minutes to prevent skewers from burning on the grill. While skewers are soaking, preheat the grill to 375 degrees.
2. Chop chicken breasts into chunks and chop fresh rosemary and mince the garlic cloves.
3. Bring together all ingredients in a wide mixing bowl and stir and coat the chicken chunks thoroughly.
4. Arrange the chicken chunks evenly on the 8 skewers. Cover and refrigerate chicken skewers until ready to grill.
5. Then grill the kabobs for 3 minutes on each side for a total of 12 to 15 minutes. Cook chicken thoroughly.

Spicy Deviled Eggs

Total Prep & Cooking Time: 20 min.
Yields: 6 servings
Nutrition Facts: Calories: 153| Protein: 5.9g | Net Carbs: 5.7g | Fat 12g

Ingredients:

- 6 eggs
- 1 tbsp. red curry paste
- ½ cup mayonnaise
- ¼ tsp. salt
- ½ tbsp. poppy seeds

Method:

1. Cover eggs with water in an appropriately sized pan and bring to a boil without a lid.
2. Simmer the eggs for about 8 minutes and then cool quickly with ice-cold water.
3. Remove the eggs from the shells. Then cut eggs in half and subtract the yellow yolks and transfer the yolks in a little bowl.
4. Put the egg halves on a serving platter plate and let cool in the refrigerator.
5. In the same bowl, mix the curry paste, mayonnaise, and egg yolks into a smooth paste. Add salt to taste.
6. Take the egg whites from the refrigerator and add the batter to the center of the eggs. Scatter sesame seeds on the eggs for garnish.

Bacon Avocado Bombs

Total Prep & Cooking Time: 20 min.
Yields: 4 servings
Nutrition Facts: Calories: 153| Protein: 5.9g | Net Carbs: 5.7g | Fat 12g

Ingredients:
- 2 avocados
- 1/3 cups shredded cheddar
- 8 slices bacon

Method:
1. Heat the broiler and line a small baking sheet with foil.
2. Slice each avocado in half, detach the center pits and unpeel the skin.
3. Fill 2 halves of the avocado with cheese and then top with other halves. Then wrap each avocado with 4 slices of bacon.
4. Put the bacon-wrapped avocados on the cooking sheet and broil for
5. 5 minutes or until bacon is at preferred crispiness. Carefully flip the avocados with tongs and cook for an additional five minutes.
6. Cut in half and serve.

Cauliflower Mac & Cheese

Total Prep & Cooking Time: 5 min.
Yields: 1 serving
Nutrition Facts: Calories: 128| Protein: 9.4g | Net Carbs: 4.8g | Fat 14.9g

Ingredients:

- ¾ cup frozen cauliflower florets
- 1 oz. shredded cheddar cheese
- 1 tbsp. heavy cream

Method:

1. Using a small microwavable dish with a lid, heat the cauliflower for about 1 minute.
2. Remove from microwave and then chop the cauliflower into small pieces.
3. Then microwave for another 50 seconds and add shredded cheese on top.
4. Microwave for an extra 10 seconds to melt the shredded cheese.
5. Add in heavy cream and stir until creamy sauce forms.

Everything Bagel Keto Fat Bombs

Total Prep & Cooking Time: 10 min.
Yields: 18 servings
Nutrition Facts: Calories: 60| Protein: 2g | Net Carbs: 1g | Fat 5g

Ingredients:

- 8 oz. cream cheese, softened
- 1/3 cup everything seasoning
- 1 tsp. dried dill
- 2 tbsp. chives, chopped
- Pepper and salt as desired
- 4 oz. smoked salmon, chopped

Method:

1. Chop up the chives and slice the salmon.
2. Using a hand mixer, beat the cream cheese.
3. Then throw in the chives, dill, and seasonings in a bowl and continue to mix smoothly on average speed. Slowly, blend in the smoked salmon and salt to taste.
4. Cover baking sheet with wax paper. Scoop out bite-sized balls and cool in the refrigerator for 30 minutes.
5. Take scoops out of the refrigerator and put everything seasoning on a plate.
6. Quickly roll each fat bomb in a ball and then roll them into the everything seasoning. Continue rolling, so the seasoning sticks to the bombs.
7. Enjoy now or chill for later.

Mozzarella Stuffed Meatballs

Total Prep & Cooking Time: 40 min.
Yields: 4 servings
Nutrition Facts: Calories: 396| Protein: 59.6g | Net Carbs: 1g | Fat 15.6g

Ingredients:
- 1 ½ lbs. ground beef
- 1 tbsp. dried basil
- Butter for frying
- 4 oz. mozzarella cheese
- Pepper and salt as desired
- 2 tbsp. cold water

Method:
1. Combine the ground beef, basil, cold water, salt, and pepper in a sizeable bowl. Stir completely with a big wooden utensil or using your hands.
2. Make 10 flat patties about 3-4 inches wide and ½ thick.
3. Then cut the mozzarella into 10 pieces and put in the middle of each beef patty. Roll the meat around cheese in your hands to form a ball.
4. Fry each meatball in butter over medium heat until juices are clear.

Prosciutto-wrapped salmon skewers

Total Prep & Cooking Time: 25 min.
Yields: 4 servings
Nutrition Facts: Calories: 340| Protein: 45g | Net Carbs: 1.7g | Fat 16.6g

Ingredients:
- 8 wooden skewers
- ¼ cup fresh basil, finely chopped
- 1 lb. salmon, frozen
- 3 ½ oz. prosciutto, sliced
- Pepper
- 1 tbsp. olive oil

Method:
1. Soak the skewers in water so they do not burn when cooking. Finely chop the basil. Then sprinkle the basil with pepper to taste.
2. Cut the almost thawed salmon filets length-wise and then slide the length-wise salmon.
3. Then rotate the salmon skewers in the finely chopped basil and pepper.
4. Thinly slice the prosciutto and enclose it tightly around the salmon.
5. Lightly splash olive oil on skewers and fry in a skillet, bake in the oven or cook on the grill. Cook salmon all the way through.

Nacho Cheese Crisps

Total Prep & Cooking Time: 55 min.
Yields: 6 servings
Nutrition Facts: Calories: 340| Protein: 45g | Net Carbs: 1.7g | Fat 16.6g

Ingredients:
- 1 8 oz. package sliced cheddar
- 2 tsp. taco seasoning

Method:
1. Switch on the oven to 250 degrees.
2. Cut each slice of cheese into 9 squares. Then place them in the mixing bowl. Add taco seasoning on cheese squares and coat thoroughly.
3. Cover baking sheet with wax paper. Lay the cheese slices evenly (no overlapping).
4. Bake for 40 minutes so that the cheese is crispy and golden. Let cool 10 minutes and then remove from parchment paper.

CHAPTER 4 DESSERTS

Delectable, sweet, and savory, give in to your sweet tooth with these delicious dessert recipes.

Oven-Baked Brie

Total Prep & Cooking Time: 15 min.
Yields: 4 servings
Nutrition Facts: Calories: 346| Protein: 14.9g | Net Carbs: 3.1g | Fat 31.4g

Ingredients:
- 9 oz. Brie cheese
- Pepper and salt as desired
- 1 tbsp. fresh rosemary, chopped
- 1 garlic clove, minced
- 1 tbsp. olive oil
- 2 oz. pecans, chopped

Method:
1. Mince the garlic and coarsely chop the rosemary and pecans. Switch on the oven to 400 degrees.
2. Arrange cheese on a cooking sheet covered in wax paper or a small non-stick baking dish.
3. Mix the garlic, rosemary, pecans, and olive oil in a small mixing bowl. Add pepper and salt as desired.
4. Spread and smooth the nut mixture on the brie cheese. Bake for 10 minutes to make the cheese soft, and make sure the nuts are toasted. Serve warm.

Lemon Ice Cream

Total Prep & Cooking Time: 1 hr. 30 min.
Yields: 6 servings
Nutrition Facts: Calories: 256| Protein: 4.1g | Net Carbs: 15.3g | Fat 26.2g

Ingredients:
- 1 lemon, juice and zest
- 1/3 erythritol
- 3 eggs
- 1 ¾ heavy whipping cream
- ¼ tsp. yellow food coloring

Method:
1. Rinse the lemon in lukewarm water and finely grate the peel to make the lemon zest. Then squeeze the lemon juice in a bowl and set aside.
2. Split the yellow egg yolks and egg whites. Thrash the egg whites until they are stiff.
3. In a different bowl, whisk the egg yolks and sweetener together until fluffy and light. Add lemon juice and few drops of yellow food coloring to the mixture to the yolk mixture.
4. Then delicately crease the egg whites into the yolk combination.
5. In a large bowl, whip the heavy cream until peaks form. Then lightly blend the egg combination into the cream.
6. Pour mixture into ice cream maker and freeze, follow your machine's specific instructions to create the ice cream properly.
7. If you don't have an ice cream machine, then place the bowl of mixture in the freezer and stir well every half hour with a spatula. Keep in the freezer for 2 hours or until it reaches your desired consistency.

Chocolate Lava Cake

Total Prep & Cooking Time: 15 min.
Yields: 2 servings
Nutrition Facts: Calories: 460| Protein: 11.7g | Net Carbs: 3.4g | Fat 43.3g

Ingredients:

- 2 oz. dark chocolate
- 1 tbsp. superfine almond flour
- 2 oz. unsalted butter for cake
- 2 eggs
- 2 tbsp

Method:

1. Switch on the oven to 350 degrees and grease 2 ramekins with butter.
2. Then melt the chocolate and 2 oz. butter. Stir well to combine.
3. Using a mixer, beat the eggs well. Then add the beaten eggs, almond flour, and sweetener into chocolate mixture. Stir well until you get a dough-like consistency, and it pours easily.
4. Distribute batter evenly into the 2 ramekins. Bake for 9 minutes and the top is still jiggly. Be careful not to over bake.
5. Turnout gently onto plates, and you can serve with your favorite toppings.

Low Carb Snickerdoodle Cookies

Total Prep & Cooking Time: 25 min.
Yields: 16 servings
Nutrition Facts: Calories: 131 | Protein: 3g | Net Carbs: 1.5g | Fat 13g

Ingredients:

Cookies:
- 2 cups superfine almond flour
- ½ tsp. baking soda
- ¾ cup erythritol sweetener
- ½ cup salted butter softened
- Salt

Coating:
- 1 tsp. ground cinnamon
- 2 tbsp. erythritol

Method:
1. Switch on oven to 350 degrees.
2. Combine all the ingredients until you form a stiff dough.
3. Then roll the cookie dough into 16 equal-sized balls, about 1 ½ inches wide.
4. Mix the sweetener and cinnamon in a small bowl to create the coating.
5. Then roll the balls generously in the cinnamon coating.
6. Place the coated cookie balls on a cookie sheet covered in parchment paper. Then gently smash with a flat round surface.
7. Bake for 15 minutes and then let cool before serving.

Low Carb Peanut Butter Cookies

Total Prep & Cooking Time: 25 min.
Yields: 27 Servings
Nutrition Facts: Calories: 94 Protein: 4g | Net Carbs: 2g | Fat 7g

Ingredients:
- 2 large eggs
- ½ cup erythritol
- 1 ¼ cup creamy peanut butter
- ¾ cup peanuts
- ¼ tsp. Salt

Method:
1. Crush the peanuts and set aside. Preheat the oven to 350 degrees and use a cookie sheet covered with parchment paper.
2. Combine eggs, sweetener, salt and creamy peanut butter in a blender or food processor. Manage until smooth and clean offsides when mixture sticks.
3. Toss in crushed peanuts and join with other ingredients. Leave some crunch for texture.
4. Scoop the dough into spheres and place on baking sheet. Press the dough using a fork to create crosshatch top. Wipe fork with water before using it again.
5. Bake for 15-20 minutes until golden brown and crunchy.

No Bake Coconut Bars

Total Prep & Cooking Time: 30 min.
Yields: 6 servings
Nutrition Facts: Calories: 239| Protein: 2.7g | Net Carbs: 18.7g | Fat 19.5g

Ingredients:
- 1 cup dark chocolate chips
- ½ almond butter
- 1 tbsp. coconut oil
- 2 ½ cups coconut, shredded
- 1 tbsp. monk fruit (or sticky sweetener)

Method:
1. Combine coconut oil, monk fruit, almond butter, shredded coconut, in a food processor and handle until all sticks together easily.
2. Cover a baking pan with wax paper and layer the coconut mix evenly. Pressing to compact.
3. Melt the chocolate in the microwave and the spread on top of coconut dough.
4. Freeze for 20 minutes until hard. Then cut into squares.

Peanut Butter Chocolate Fat Bombs

Total Prep & Cooking Time: 30 min.
Yields: 16 servings
Nutrition Facts: Calories: 291| Protein: 5g | Net Carbs: 5g | Fat 28g

Ingredients:
- 8 oz. cream cheese, softened
- ½ cup keto-friendly peanut butter
- ¼ cup coconut oil and 2 tbsp.
- ¼ keto-friendly dark chocolate chips
- ¼ tsp. kosher salt

Method:
1. Combine the peanut butter, cream cheese, ¼ cup coconut oil, kosher salt. Use a hand mixer to beat the mixture for 2 minutes or until thoroughly mixed.
2. Leave the dessert in the freezer for 10 to 15 minutes or until the combination stiffens. While the mixture is in the freezer, line a cooking sheet with wax paper.
3. When mixture is firm, take it out of the freezer and use a scoop or spoon to create tablespoon-sized balls. Put in the refrigerator for about 5 minutes to harden balls.
4. While the mixture is in the refrigerator, make the chocolate drizzle. Combine the chocolate chips and remaining coconut oil into a microwave-safe bowl. Warm up chocolate in 30-second intervals until melted.
5. Then drizzle over the peanut butter fat bombs on the baking sheet. Keep in the refrigerator for 5 minutes to solidify the chocolate.

Cookie Dough Fat Bombs

Total Prep & Cooking Time: 65 min.
Yields: 30 servings
Nutrition Facts: Calories: 70| Protein: 2g | Net Carbs: 2g | Fat 7g

Ingredients:
- 8 tbsp. (1 stick) butter softened
- 2 cups almond flour
- ½ tsp. pure vanilla extract
- 2/3 cups keto-friendly dark chocolate chips
- ½ tsp. kosher salt
- 1/3 cup keto friendly confectioners' sugar

Method:
1. Use a hand mixer to heat butter until light and fluffy. Then combine the confectioners' sugar, vanilla, and salt with butter. Then beat until well combined.
2. Slowly pour in almond flour until thoroughly mixed, and no dry spots remain. Then fold chocolate chips into the batter.
3. Enclose the bowl with plastic wrap and position in refrigerator for 15 to 20 minutes to firm dough.
4. Use a small spoon to scoop dough and roll the dough into small balls.
5. Store the cookie dough bombs in the refrigerator up to 1 week or in the freezer for up to a month.

White Chocolate Raspberry Fat Bombs

Total Prep & Cooking Time: 65 min.
Yields: 10- 12 servings
Nutrition Facts: Calories: 70| Protein: 2g | Net Carbs: 2g | Fat 7g

Ingredients:
- ½ cup coconut oil
- 2 oz. cacao butter
- ½ cup freeze-dried raspberries
- ¼ powdered erythritol sweetener

Method:
1. Put paper liners into a 12 cup muffin pan or use a silicone muffin pan with no liners.
2. In a small saucepan, heat coconut oil and cacao butter over the lowest setting until completely melted. Then remove the saucepan from the heat.
3. Use a food processor, blender, or coffee grinder to blend the freeze-dried raspberries.
4. Add the blended berries and sweetener to the saucepan and then stir until sweetener is dissolved.
5. Evenly divide the mixture into the muffin cups. Keep stirring mixture while pouring into the cups. The raspberry mixture will sink to the bottom.
6. Chill in the refrigerator for 1 hour or until firm.

Made in the USA
Coppell, TX
19 December 2020